JUMP!

KANGAROOS

Lynette Robbins

PowerKiDS
press
New York

For Kate and her (toy) kangaroo, Victoria

Published in 2012 by The Rosen Publishing Group, Inc.
29 East 21st Street, New York, NY 10010

First Edition

Editor: Joanne Randolph
Book Design: Ashley Drago and Erica Clendening

Photo Credits: Cover, p. 17 (top) © Martin Ruegner/age fotostock; p. 4 © www.iStockphoto.com/ Michael Sacco; p. 5 © www.iStockphoto.com/MaXPdia; pp. 6, 7 (bottom), 9, 17 (bottom), 21, Shutterstock.com; p. 7 (top) John White Photos/Getty Images; p. 8 © www.iStockphoto.com/Andrew Halsall; p. 10 Joel Sartore/Getty Images; p. 11 Anup Shah/Digital Vision/Thinkstock; pp. 12–13 John W. Banagan/Getty Images; pp. 14, 22 © www.iStockphoto.com/John Carnemolla; p. 15 Theo Allofs/ Getty Images; p. 16 Hemera Technologies/Photos.com/Thinkstock; p. 18 Jason Edwards/Getty Images; p. 19 Hemera/Thinkstock; p. 20 AlexandraPhotos/Getty Images.

Library of Congress Cataloging-in-Publication Data

Robbins, Lynette.
  Kangaroos / by Lynette Robbins. — 1st ed.
      p. cm. — (Jump!)
  Includes index.
  ISBN 978-1-4488-5013-6 (library binding) — ISBN 978-1-4488-5159-1 (pbk.) —
  ISBN 978-1-4488-5160-7 (6-pack)
  1. Kangaroos—Juvenile literature. I. Title. II. Series.
  QL737.M35R628 2012
  599.2'22—dc22

                            2010047318

Manufactured in the United States of America

CPSIA Compliance Information: Batch #WS11PK: For Further Information contact Rosen Publishing, New York, New York at 1-800-237-9932

Contents

Hello, Kangaroo!

Do you know what a kangaroo is? Kangaroos are **marsupials**. Marsupials are a kind of **mammal** that carries its young in a pouch. Kangaroos are also some of the best jumpers on Earth. A large kangaroo can easily jump over a 10-foot (3 m) fence!

Wallabies are small kangaroos. All kangaroos are marsupials, and all marsupials carry their babies in pouches, as this one is doing.

Kangaroos are macropods. "Macropod" means "big feet." This is a great way to describe kangaroos. Their feet can be up to 18 inches (46 cm) long! A kangaroo needs such big feet to jump. A jumping kangaroo moves very fast. Are you ready to jump into the world of this hopping marsupial?

Here a group of kangaroos hops its way across an Australian plain. Can you see how long their back legs are? Their long legs make them powerful jumpers.

Lots of Kangaroos

When you think about kangaroos, you likely think about one of the four **species** of large kangaroos. The largest kangaroo is the red kangaroo. There are two kinds of gray kangaroos. They are the eastern gray kangaroo and the western gray kangaroo. The fourth kind is the antilopine kangaroo.

Red kangaroos can grow to be around 5 feet (1.5 m) tall. Their tails are about 3 feet (1 m) long.

LEFT: Yellow-footed rock wallabies are small macropods that like to live in rocky places.

BELOW: Gray kangaroos generally live in wetter places than red kangaroos. They spend more time in places with trees, too, which gives them the nickname the forester kangaroo.

There are also more than 50 other marsupials in the kangaroo family. Wallaroos are a little smaller than kangaroos. Wallabies are smaller than wallaroos. There are also tree kangaroos, which hop from one tree to another. The smallest kind of kangaroo is the rat kangaroo.

Home, Hopping Home

The large species of kangaroos live in Australia. Many small kangaroos live there as well. In fact, there are more kangaroos in Australia than people! Some smaller kangaroo species also live on islands near Australia, including New Guinea. Most kangaroos live in the Australian **Outback**, on grassy plains or in dry deserts. Kangaroos can live where it does not rain very often.

These red kangaroos live on the grassy plains of Australia's Outback.

It is very hot in Australia. Kangaroos spend most of the hot day resting in the shade. Sometimes they dig holes that they can lie in to stay cool. Kangaroos are **nocturnal.** That means they are more active at night, when it is cooler.

This kangaroo is taking a nap in the hot afternoon sun. Once the sun starts to go down, kangaroos get busy looking for food.

Huge Hind Legs

.Kangaroos have large, strong legs. Kangaroos cannot move their legs one at a time. They must move them both together. That means that they cannot walk or run, as other animals can. They must jump! Jumping does not slow them down, though.

When they are in danger, male red kangaroos can jump a length of up to 45 feet (14 m).

Larger kangaroos can move at speeds of 30 miles per hour (48 km/h). A kangaroo that is jumping across a plain can cover 15 feet (5 m) in one bound!

Red and gray kangaroos are about 5 to 6 feet (1.5–2 m) tall. That is about as tall as an adult person. Kangaroos also have long tails, which they use for balance. They have small heads with long ears.

Kangaroos use their front legs to crawl-walk when grazing. To do this, the kangaroo uses its tail and front legs to hold its body up as it lifts its back legs forward.

Kangaroo Quick Facts

1

A male kangaroo is called a buck. Australians sometimes call a male kangaroo a boomer, jack, or an old man. A female kangaroo is called a doe. Australians sometimes call a female a flyer or a jill.

5

Most of the time, a female kangaroo has a baby, or joey, inside her body that is waiting to be born, a baby **developing** in her pouch, and a joey that has just left the pouch.

6

Kangaroos are very social animals. They spend a lot of time using their front paws to pick out dirt, small insects, and dead skin from each other's fur.

7

Kangaroos **communicate** with each other through coughs, hisses, growls, and other sounds. A mother kangaroo makes a clicking sound to call her joey.

2

Kangaroos have two kinds of teeth. The teeth at the front of their mouths work like scissors to cut the grass that they eat. The teeth at the back are used for chewing. New back teeth grow in as they get worn out.

3

Bacteria help break down a kangaroo's food inside its stomach. Cows and sheep also have bacteria inside their stomachs.

4

Kangaroos can go for a long time without drinking water. They get much of the water they need from the plants that they eat.

8

Kangaroos can live for up to 20 years in a zoo. In the wild, most kangaroos live for only 6 to 8 years.

Time to Eat

Kangaroos are **herbivores**. This means they eat only plants. Kangaroos that live on the plains or in the desert eat mostly grasses and roots. It takes a long time for kangaroos to get enough food. They spend from 7 to 14 hours a day eating!

Grass is hard to **digest**, so kangaroos chew their food two times. First a kangaroo

If kangaroos can find the right foods, they do not need to drink often. However, if they find water, they will stop to take a sip.

chews its food with its flat back teeth and swallows it. Then wads of food are forced from its stomach back into the kangaroo's mouth and chewed again. When it is swallowed the second time, the food goes to a different part of the kangaroo's stomach.

This western gray kangaroo is eating a banksia flower. Banksia trees grow in woodlands in a few places in western Australia.

Watch Out for Dingoes

Dingoes are kangaroos' main **predators**. Dingoes are wild dogs. They often pick a young kangaroo as **prey**. They sometimes hunt adult females, too, because they are smaller than males.

Dingoes hunt kangaroos in packs. A pack of dingoes may come at a kangaroo from many different directions

Dingoes sometimes hunt alone. They often work together to hunt larger animals, such as kangaroos, though.

at once. Sometimes one dingo chases a kangaroo toward the rest of the pack. Kangaroos fight back by kicking with their powerful hind legs. A kangaroo's toes have sharp claws. One powerful kick from a kangaroo can kill a dingo.

Life in a Mob

Kangaroos live in groups, called mobs. A mob may have as few as 3 kangaroos or as many as 50. It is safer for kangaroos to live in mobs than it is for them to live alone. Some kangaroos in the mob act as lookouts. When a kangaroo senses danger, it thumps the ground hard! Then all the kangaroos hop away in different directions.

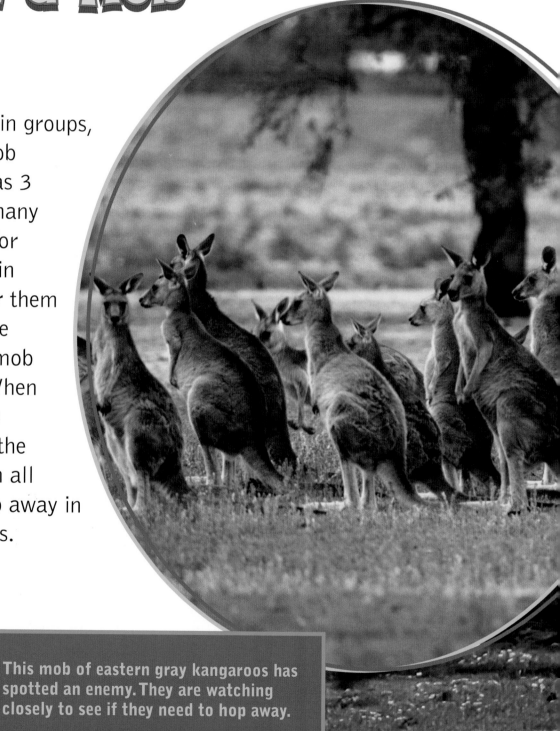

This mob of eastern gray kangaroos has spotted an enemy. They are watching closely to see if they need to hop away.

The largest and strongest male is the leader of the mob. He gets to mate with most of the other females in the mob. That means that he is the father of most of the babies, called joeys. Male kangaroos fight to see which will get to be the leader.

Kangaroos will hop a long way to find food. They will also jump quickly away at the first sign of danger.

Life in a Pouch

Do you remember that a kangaroo is a marsupial? Marsupials are different from other mammals. Their babies are born much earlier than other mammals' are. A newborn kangaroo is smaller than a lima bean and does not look like a kangaroo at all! It is only partly formed. A newborn kangaroo must use its front paws to pull itself up its mother's

This joey still spends a lot of time in its mother's pouch. Soon it will be too big to return, though.

body and into the pouch. Once inside, it begins to drink its mother's milk. Milk helps the baby grow and develop.

After about six months, the baby will be big enough to come out of the pouch. Even after a joey can come out of its mother's pouch, it still returns often. At about 10 months old, it leaves the pouch for good.

A mother kangaroo can have a newborn kangaroo in her pouch even while she is still caring for an older joey. This happens only when there is plenty of food, though.

Kangaroos Forever!

Most kangaroos stay away from people. However, kangaroos can cause trouble for farmers. Sometimes kangaroos hop over fences and eat grass that was meant for sheep and cattle. People are allowed to hunt kangaroos. However, only a certain number of kangaroos can be hunted each year. Kangaroo meat is used for pet food and is sometimes eaten by people. Kangaroo hides are used to make shoes, bags, and soccer balls.

Kangaroos are interesting animals that have adapted, or changed, to suit their special home. When people think of Australia, they think of these wonderful animals!

Most Australians like kangaroos. In fact, there is even a kangaroo on the Australian **coat of arms**! Other people like kangaroos, too. People come from all over the world to see them bounding across the Outback!

Glossary

bacteria (bak-TIR-ee-uh) Tiny living things that cannot be seen with the eye alone. Some bacteria cause illness or rotting, but others are helpful.

coat of arms (KOHT UV AHRMZ) A picture, on and around a shield or on a drawing of a shield, which stands for a family or a country.

communicate (kuh-MYOO-nih-kayt) To share facts or feelings.

developing (dih-VEH-lup-ing) Changing and growing.

digest (dy-JEST) To break down food so that the body can use it.

herbivores (ER-buh-vorz) Animals that eat only plants.

mammal (MA-mul) A warm-blooded animal that has a backbone and hair, breathes air, and feeds milk to its young.

marsupials (mahr-SOO-pee-ulz) Animals that carry their young in pouches.

nocturnal (nok-TUR-nul) Active during the night.

Outback (OWT-bak) Wilderness in Australia.

predators (PREH-duh-terz) Animals that kill other animals for food.

prey (PRAY) An animal that is hunted by another animal for food.

species (SPEE-sheez) One kind of living thing. All people are one species.

Index

Web Sites

Due to the changing nature of Internet links, PowerKids Press has developed an online list of Web sites related to the subject of this book. This site is updated regularly. Please use this link to access the list:
www.powerkidslinks.com/jump/kangaroo/